LEARNING TO FLY
RADIO CONTROL HELICOPTERS

Learning To Fly Radio Control Helicopters

Dave Day

ARGUS BOOKS

Argus Books

Argus House
Boundary Way
Hemel Hempstead
Hertfordshire HP2 7ST
England

First published by Argus Books 1990

© Argus Books 1990

ISBN 1 85486 025 9

Phototypesetting by GCS, Leighton Buzzard
Printed and bound in Great Britain by
William Clowes Ltd, Beccles

Contents

Chapter 1
Introduction

THE PURPOSE of this book is to explain how to fly model radio controlled helicopters. In many ways it is an abbreviated version of my earlier work *Flying Model Helicopters*, which I recommend for those who require a fuller appreciation of the subject. However, many passages have been updated, or changed to reflect modern thinking, in accordance with my greater experience of a wider range of model types.

I give little coverage to the associated subject of the setting up of the model. Here, you are recommended to consult the companion volume in this series, *Setting up R/C Helicopters.*

To those who are new to this absorbing –and highly addictive – branch of the model hobby, I cannot repeat too often that the two essential ingredients for success are dogged persistence and experienced help.

Good luck!

Chapter 2
Radio control equipment

Standard or helicopter radio

ONE OF THE first things you must consider when producing your first R/C helicopter is which type of radio equipment to use. Radio equipment is available in two basic types – aircraft and helicopter. Other special types are available in some cases to cater for specific applications but these need not concern us in this book.

The main difference between the two types is that the helicopter radio will have two separate channels for the throttle and collective pitch controls which will both be operated by one axis of a control stick. There will, therefore, be a minimum of five channels required. This inevitably means that a helicopter set will cost a little more than a basic aircraft set which needs no more than four channels.

Your decision here will obviously depend to some extent on whether you already have an aircraft radio and just how much you are prepared to spend on your first model. *Any* model helicopter *can* be flown with a basic 4-channel aircraft set, but it will be more difficult to set up and very limited in terms of just what you will be able to do with the model, once you have learned to fly it. This latter point is a very important one since, until you have learned to fly, you don't really *need* a helicopter radio.

Another point concerns the nature of the model. Model helicopters can be obtained in two forms – those with variable pitch rotor blades and those with fixed pitch blades. Fixed pitch models are much simpler but were, at one time, almost in danger of disappearing until their attraction as a cheap means of learning to fly was realised. They only need a basic 4-channel radio to fly them and, if you already possess such a set, have much to commend them.

If you are starting completely from scratch, however, and have the cash available, I recommend that you purchase a basic helicopter radio which can

The *Micro-mold* 'Lark' is an early example of a fixed pitch machine. Note the very simple mechanical layout. This produces a machine which is easy to repair and ideal for the beginner.

The latest *Schlüter* machine is the 'Magic', which has very complex mechanics and a high all-up weight – 11½ lb in this case. *Schlüter/Webra* motor has excellent performance, but high compression can give starting problems.

still be used with a fixed pitch machine if required, but will be of great help if a variable (collective) pitch machine is purchased.

Before I move on to a fuller description of helicopter radios, let's summarise the above:

● *Any* machine can be flown with a basic 4-channel radio control outfit ('aircraft' set).

● Fixed pitch machines only *need* four channels anyway.

● While there are advantages in the use of a 5-channel 'helicopter' radio on collective pitch machines, these are not apparent until you have learned to fly.

Controls found in helicopter radios and their use

Apart from the additional pitch channel, a basic helicopter will also have the following *minimum* features:

1. Some means of 'freezing' the throttle channel in a preset position ('Throttle Hold' switch). This is used when practising autorotation landings (see Chapter 8).

2. A device for raising the engine speed when the throttle/pitch stick is in the 'low' position ('Idle Up' switch) (Fig. 2.1). This is used when performing aerobatics (see Chapter 9).
3. A tail compensation system (ATS) which changes the tail rotor trim to compensate for changes in motor power (torque) (Fig. 2.2).
4. Most basic sets also now include a means of adjusting the extremes of the pitch channel range ('End Point' adjustment). This will not affect the throttle channel (Fig. 2.3).

More complex – and expensive – sets will have end point adjustment on all channels, complex 'tailoring' of the pitch and throttle channel movement, including two 'idle up' settings with different pitch ranges, various combinations of mixing and coupling aimed at making the model easier to fly and suitable for contest requirements, etc. The very latest equipment features computer programming of all the above, with the capability to memorise all the parameters for several different models. This is just the icing on the cake. Items 1 to 4 above are the basic essentials.

Typical of the hi-tech 'top-of-the-range' radio is this *JR* 'PCM-10', which features many programmable options in the transmitter and can store settings for seven different models.

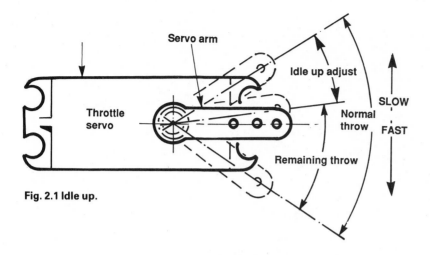

Servo arm

Idle up adjust

Throttle servo

Normal throw

SLOW

FAST

Remaining throw

Fig. 2.1 Idle up.

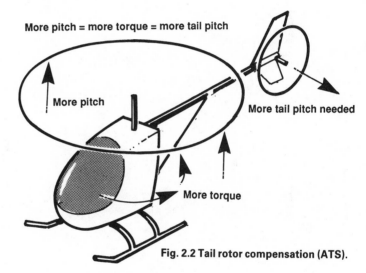

More pitch = more torque = more tail pitch

More pitch

More tail pitch needed

More torque

Fig. 2.2 Tail rotor compensation (ATS).

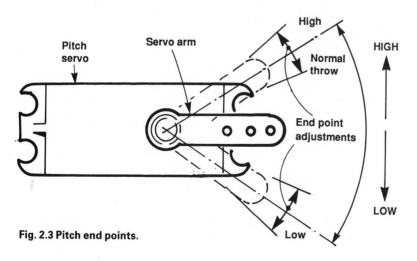

Pitch servo

Servo arm

High

HIGH

Normal throw

End point adjustments

Low

LOW

Fig. 2.3 Pitch end points.

Chapter 3
Gyrostabilisers

Don't expect the impossible

A GYROSTABILISER consists of a small, rapidly spinning, motor-driven flywheel which is able to sense movement of a model about any chosen axis and apply a cancelling movement to the appropriate servo. This description is deliberately chosen to be non-specific, since a gyro stabiliser can be used on *any* axis of any type of model. For reasons which need not concern us here, they have become almost solely used on the tail rotor servo of model helicopters to assist in controlling the tail and are known as tail rotor gyros or just 'gyros'.

Note that the word used was to 'assist' in controlling the tail. There are still many people who think (perhaps a better word is 'hope'!) that a gyro can do *all* the work of controlling the tail and thus leave the pilot free to concentrate on other things. A moment's thought will show that this ideal state cannot possibly exist, since a gyro cannot react to something until *after* that something has already happened. This means that even the best of gyros will always be a little too late to *prevent* any unwanted movement. Note, too, that once a particular movement has become established, the gyro will try to preserve it.

What a gyro *does* do, however, is to *damp out* unwanted movements and allow the pilot more time to react. It is worth pointing out that virtually all of the current best model helicopter pilots learned to fly them before the existence of a practical gyrostabiliser. They did it 'the hard way' and so can anyone else with sufficient determination. The gyro has made it much easier to learn to fly but, once you overcome the basic hurdle, it merely serves to smooth things out and make your flying tidier.

Typical installation in *Kalt* 'Baron 20 MX'. Receiver is attached to battery with servo tape – rubber bands are for added security. Note very neat installation possible with British *Quest* gyro.

They are all the same, under the skin

It is amazing how the model world can come up with numerous variations on the same basic device. A basic gyro-stabiliser consists of the flywheel and its motor, plus an electronics package. This is inserted between the receiver and the tail rotor servo. In many cases, there will be a second lead to be plugged into the receiver which will enable the gain, or sensitivity, of the gyro electronics to be varied from the transmitter. Here we come to the first of many possible variations, in that this change of gain may be continuously variable or switched between two different values. These two values can usually be varied by controls mounted on the gyro itself or, in some cases, also changed at the transmitter.

While some types require a separate battery, most can be powered by the same battery that is used for the receiver and servos. However, where a single battery is used to power both the radio equipment *and* the gyro motor, the battery pack normally supplied with the radio equipment will not have sufficient capacity to give a reasonable safety margin. A typical pack will have a capacity of 500 mAH which, in a collective pitch model employing five servos and a gyro, may have a fully charged life of only 20–25 minutes and certainly no more than 1 hour.

Most manufacturers are able to supply a larger capacity battery for this purpose. This will normally have a capacity of 1000 or 1200 mAH. Even when this is used, it is not advisable to expect a safe endurance of more than about an hour.

The abbreviation 'mAH' used above stands for milliamphours. A battery of 500 mAH capacity can supply a current of 50 milliamps (mA) for 10 hours (H) or 500 for 1 hour, etc.

Make sure that it is helping!

One essential requirement, before attempting to fly a model equipped with a gyro for the first time, is to ensure that the gyro is working in the correct sense. This means that, if the tail of your model starts to swing towards the left, then the gyro must apply a correction which will make the tail move to the right. If not, the gyro will merely aggravate any instability in the model and produce a situation which is beyond the control of any normal pilot.

The overall response of the model to a given control input at the transmitter can be varied in several ways. A purely mechanical variation can be effected by changing the relative lengths of the servo arm and the tail rotor pitch control lever. Increasing the length of the servo arm or reducing the length of the pitch lever will give increased response.

Many modern radio control outfits will allow this response to be varied from the transmitter as already described. Here you simply ensure that the mechanical linkage will give more than sufficient control and then adjust the radio transmitter to suit. Note that the transmitter control will only allow you to *reduce* the response; it cannot give more throw than the mechanical linkage will allow. Also note that the gyro gain control is similarly limited by the mechanical linkage and this too can only *reduce* the response.

The novice flyer will normally require that the model's response to the transmitter is at a minimum, to avoid any tendency to overcontrol, while the gyro has as much effect as possible to help him during the learning process.

You must be wary of two possible pitfalls here:

1. The mechanical linkage is set to give a very large control range which is

then reduced to manageable proportions by means of the transmitter throw adjustment. This still gives the gyro an oversensitive control and it will be very difficult to set the gyro gain control to give an acceptable response. An overcontrolling gyro will cause the tail to oscillate. In this situation, it may be necessary to reduce the gyro gain to such an extent to cure the oscillation that the gyro has little, if any, effect at all.

2. Conversely, if the model's sensitivity is reduced mechanically to make it easy to fly, the gyro may be left with insufficient control to have any effect.

Both of these situations lead to the conclusion that the gyro is inadequate for its purpose, whereas the real problem lies in the adjustment of the model's control linkage. This is where experienced help is worth its weight in gold, since the correct set-up can only be established by flying the model and adjusting the linkages and controls to give correct gyro action and *then* setting the tail up to suit the particular flyer.

This one point alone has almost certainly caused many novice flyers to struggle on with an unmanageable model which could easily be completely transformed by correct adjustment.

The *Hirobo* 'Shuttle' – a basic pod-and-boom machine – can be fitted with a GRP fuselage to produce this convincing *Bell* '222'. A very simple retracting undercarriage is also available.

Chapter 4
Hovering

First attempts

ONE OF the most common types of damage which the novice pilot is likely to inflict on his model is that caused by one of the main rotor blades coming into contact with the tailboom. An examination of any typical model will lead to the conclusion that this is not possible, since it will require an unbelievable amount of force to make the blades come anywhere near the boom. Nonetheless, the forces acting upon the model when it is unceremoniously 'dumped' onto the ground to avoid an impending crash are more than adequate to ensure that the seemingly impossible can happen with depressing regularity.

The first sign that you are making real progress in learning to fly is that such mishaps become rarer and, eventually, uncommon despite the model not having been changed in any way.

Fortunately, assuming that your model

The *Kalt* 'Cyclone' has established an enviable reputation for long life and low maintenance. The standard 0.50 powered machine makes a superb trainer. A 0.61 engine gives superb performance. Shown here with optional GRP canopy.

is a collective pitch type, it is possible to reduce the chances of this happening in the early stages by setting up the model in a suitable manner. Many manufacturers give details of how the pitch range of their models should be set up. Usually this is aimed at those who can already fly fairly competently and want to perform circuits, or even aerobatics, which means that some amount of *negative* pitch is required.

For the beginner, however, this negative pitch angle is exactly what is *not* required and it is recommended that the lowest pitch that the blades can reach should be +1°. This ensures that, if you suddenly pull the throttle stick hard back and drop the model onto the ground very hard, the blades will still be lifting and not pushing themselves down towards the tailboom. However, don't assume that this will provide a complete cure for the problem, it will merely reduce it.

Just how you go about determining the pitch angle of your blades depends to some extent on the make of helicopter which you purchase and also on the depth of your pocket. There are several devices on the market which are designed to measure the pitch angle with varying degrees of accuracy but, like everything else, the good ones are expensive. Some manufacturers supply a wood or plastic template in their kits which will enable you to set the pitch to the recommended range. If one of these is not supplied, it is not too difficult to make your own (Fig. 4.1).

Setting the blade tracking

When constructing your model, it is essential that the tips of the blades are painted in different, contrasting, colours. When you first run-up your model you should carefully observe the blade tips when the model is on the point of lifting off. It is almost certain that the tips will not be exactly in line with each other. By means of the different colours, it should be possible to decide which blade is running high and which is running low (Fig. 4.2).

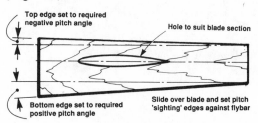

Fig. 4.1 Home made pitch gauge.

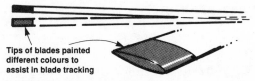

Tips of blades painted different colours to assist in blade tracking

Fig. 4.2 Blade tracking.

The pitch of each blade should be adjusted until both tips are running at exactly the same height, or tracking in exactly the same path. There are several different ways of doing this, depending on the helicopter, and you should refer to the maker's instructions for your particular model.

If you had set the pitch of the blades using a pitch gauge this will, of course, upset your careful adjustments. Here, the answer is to be extra careful with the pitch setting of one blade and make all your tracking adjustments to the *other* blade.

Some types require the 'static' tracking to be set before any running takes place. This is done by setting the model on a flat surface, measuring the height of one blade tip, then rotating the rotor head through half a turn and measuring the height of the other blade. Adjustments may then be made to ensure that both tips are at the same height above the same point *without the model being moved* (Fig. 4.3).

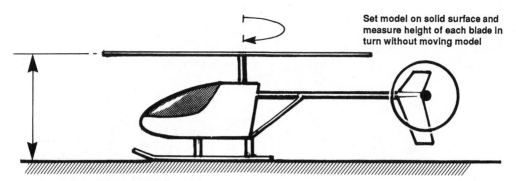

Set model on solid surface and measure height of each blade in turn without moving model

Fig. 4.3 Static tracking.

The first lift off

It cannot be repeated too often that the main ingredient required by anyone wishing to learn to fly model helicopters is sheer dogged *perseverance*! There are people in this world who have learned to fly very quickly and with little trouble, but rest assured that they are in a very small minority.

As a general rule, it can be said that those who have experience of flying fixed-wing models will find helicopters more difficult to fly than those who are starting from scratch. This is a natural result of the fact that the two types are very different and it is necessary to 'unlearn' a great deal before progress can be made.

Assuming that you have to 'go it alone', it is highly recommended that the model be fitted with floats, or some form of training undercarriage. You will find that, in the initial stages, it is much easier to control the tail if the model is always kept moving slowly forwards. If you land with forwards movement when skids are fitted, there is some danger of them 'digging in' and causing the model to tip over.

Start by increasing power until the model becomes very light on the floats but does not quite leave the ground. You will find that the model can be moved around on the ground in this state and

that all the controls are effective. Be careful not to apply too much cyclic, however, since this may still cause the model to tip over. If the model is in danger of so doing, close the throttle immediately, but smoothly. Try to avoid holding on back cyclic as the throttle is closed, since this will increase the possibility of a tailboom strike by the blades.

This is very much a two-edged sword, since the only way that the beginner can prevent the model tipping over is to close the throttle, yet any *sudden* closing of the throttle is to be avoided, for the reasons already given.

Let's have a closer look at the factors involved in the blades striking the tailboom. We have already seen that negative pitch angles should be avoided at this stage. However, even at positive angles, a sudden closing of the throttle followed by the model striking the ground can deflect the blades far enough to cause contact. A fairly common situation occurs where the model is moving forwards and the stick is pulled back to stop it, followed by the model hitting the ground in a tail down attitude. Here, the blades are already being depressed at the rear of the disc by the stick deflection (Fig. 4.4) and the tailboom is being suddenly forced upwards by striking the ground. In this situation, contact can occur with the

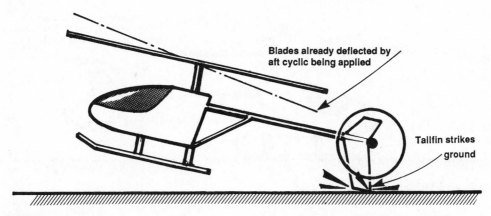

Fig. 4.4 Tailboom strike.

throttle set at hovering power and the blades at a high pitch angle and lifting strongly.

The thing to remember here is that the throttle should *never* be closed *suddenly*. Even in an emergency situation it should be closed *smoothly*. Whenever the model touches the ground, always try to ensure that it does so in a level, or slightly nose down, attitude.

When you are airborne

All of your early hovering attempts will be made with the model in front of you and the tail pointing towards you (Fig. 4.5). When you have mastered the hover, this will become a 'safe base' to return to when you get into difficulties. There is some danger of this position becoming the only way that you can fly the model, with other positions or attitudes becoming increasingly difficult. While you are at the stage where the model is being slid around in contact with the ground, perhaps accompanied by the odd short hop, it is advisable to try manoeuvring the model round in turns, both left and right, and also positioning the model with its nose towards you. This will pay dividends later.

After a few sessions of steering the model around on the ground in a 'zero height hover', you will reach the stage where the power can be increased in short bursts to lift the model clear of the ground for short periods. One advantage of this approach is that you become accustomed to the throttle setting which will allow the model to settle gently back to the ground rather than falling rapidly.

With increasing confidence, you should reach the point where the model can be kept in the air for lengthy periods with it moving slowly forwards and you following it. At this stage, don't be tempted to try to turn the model as this will inevitably lead you into a difficult situation with which you will not be able to cope.

The next hurdle is to stop moving forwards and keep the model stationary over one spot. Having got used to moving forwards, this can produce problems in knowing whether you are moving or not. Some form of marker on the ground is a great help here. This can be a patch of grass or bare earth, a stone, a car mat, etc., but do ensure that it is not large enough to cause problems if the model should touch it.

Stopping the model moving forwards can also be problematic. Obviously, you pull the cyclic stick back to lower the tail and impart a rearwards force to stop the forwards movement. Unfortunately,

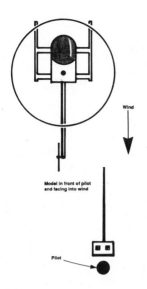

Wind

Model in front of pilot
and facing into wind

Pilot

Fig. 4.5 Safe base.

early efforts are likely to lead to the model charging backwards towards the pilot followed by a large application of *forward* stick causing an uncontrollable build up of forward speed.

Imagine that it's a pendulum

Something which may help here is to try visualising the helicopter as being on the lower end of a pendulum with the transmitter controls moving the *top* of the pendulum. Moving the top of the pendulum to, say, the right will cause the model to move to the right after a slight delay. In order to stop this movement, the top of the pendulum must now be moved sharply to the left to counteract it and then smartly back to a point directly above the helicopter at precisely the moment that the movement stops.

A model helicopter behaves in exactly the same way. If the helicopter is moving, to stop it you must apply an opposite control movement and then remove it at the precise moment that the

helicopter stops. This pendulum visualisation helped me considerably at the point where I was just about to master the hovering stage.

Setting the trim

One aspect we have not mentioned so far is the matter of model trim. Here again, experienced help is invaluable. A well trimmed model is *much* easier to fly and it is difficult for the beginner to trim a model without help.

When steering the model around on the ground, in the zero height hover, it will soon be obvious if the model has a pronounced tendency to keep heading in one direction or turning one way, and it is a simple matter to use the transmitter trim controls to correct this. Unfortunately, this trim correction may not be correct when the model leaves the ground. The solution here is to perform very short hops and observe the behaviour of the model. If the model repeatedly moves to the right, then left cyclic trim is needed and vice versa. If the model insists on moving forwards, then rear cyclic trim is needed, etc.

Tail rotor trim is variable and depends on many factors which are discussed elsewhere. At best this will always be a compromise – which explains why this is one of the most difficult aspects of learning to fly.

Go to it!

I have done my best to point out the difficulties and pitfalls associated with learning to hover but the truth is that, from here on, you are entirely on your own. Only sheer dogged persistence will finally get you there. Be warned that, once mastered, it is highly addictive.

Chapter 5
First circuits

Moving away from the hover

HAVING REACHED the point where you can hover the model consistently with its nose into wind and you standing behind it, you have established a 'safe base' position. Once you have become thoroughly familiar with this you can venture on to other things. Beware of becoming so fixated on this one position that you acquire a mental block against progressing further. This is a very real danger which can be very difficult to break out of.

Even while you are still becoming familiar with this position, you do not have to stay frozen to one spot or direction. Try walking slowly round your flying field (other flying permitting) and taking the model with you. If it is calm, there is no reason why you should not turn slowly round and walk back again. When there is a fair breeze blowing, walk very slowly backwards and take the model with you. Eventually you should be able to walk anywhere and everywhere with the model still in front of you.

From here it is a simple matter to turn slowly round and take the model round with you. The term 'tail-in circle' sounds terrifying to the beginner yet you have

A highly modified *Graupner* 'Helimax' fitted into a *GMP* 'Jetranger' body. OS.61H power. All-up weight of 10.1/4 lb. Gives a highly aerobatic machine.

just done one! Easy, wasn't it? You will have noticed the recurrent use of the word 'slowly' by now – this is the whole secret of your early departures from the static hover condition. If you allow the speed to build up you will rapidly get into a situation you cannot cope with, so take it very steadily until you become more experienced and confident. However, do not become over-confident. You need confidence in order to make any progress, yet too much, too soon, can be disastrous. The maxim, at this stage, should be 'make haste – slowly'.

The tail-in circle is very easy in flat calm conditions and becomes progressively more difficult as the wind strength increases. In windy conditions it is excellent practice in controlling the model even for the very experienced flyer. As the model presents different sides of itself to the wind, it is necessary to hold on various trim offsets to remain stationary (Fig. 5.1) relative to the pilot. Your first attempts in a light breeze will probably get no further than the crosswind point. If things start to get out of control, turn the model into wind and move it forward to the 'safe' position.

The next stage is to let the model drift slowly backwards until it is hovering alongside you or, in calm conditions, turn it until it is sideways on. If you are an experienced fixed-wing flyer, *be warned* that the latter course can be dangerous to you. Should the model start to move away, into wind, sideways, your natural inclination will be to pull the stick back to stop it. The helicopter will then back smartly into the ground!

There are two possible correct courses of action in this situation:

a. apply sideways cyclic to correct the movement; or possibly better,
b. apply tail rotor to turn the model back to the familiar hover position.

You will almost certainly find that you are happier to be seeing one side of the model than the other. Here again, don't let this situation develop until you can only fly the model on one side of you. Work at the 'bad' side until there is no difference.

Having got used to a side view, the next stage is to let the model drift slowly backwards and forwards across the wind in front of you (Fig. 5.2). Starting very gently, you increase both the speed and the sharpness of the turns as your confidence grows until you are flying a figure of eight course, still without letting the nose of the model point straight at you (Fig. 5.3).

If you have any fixed-wing experience, you will by now have realised a very important difference between helicopters and aeroplanes.

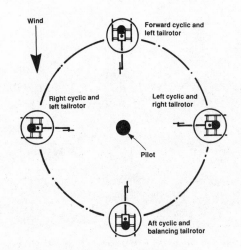

Fig. 5.1 Trim offsets during tail-in circle.

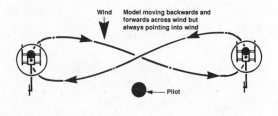

Fig. 5.2 To and fro in front of pilot.

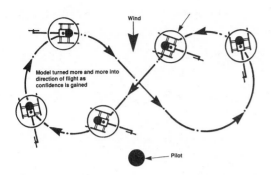

Fig. 5.3 Lazy eight.

Leave the elevator alone

When a full-sized aircraft is turned, the normal procedure is to apply a combination of rudder and aileron and then to use the elevator to maintain height. This results in a smooth 'co-ordinated' turn without any slipping or skidding. This, of course, is fine if you have an on-board pilot who can *feel* what is happening. With model aircraft, the usual method is to initiate a roll by use of the ailerons or the rudder/dihedral couple and then apply elevator to pull the model round. The result is an overbanked 'slipping' turn, but this is only apparent to the careful observer.

With a helicopter, however, the procedure is somewhat different. First, you must appreciate that a helicopter produces two different types of lift. Apart from the obvious lift produced by the rotors, which are revolving wings, there is another lift component produced by the rotor *disc* when moving forwards through the air (like a sort of flat, circular, wing). This is known as 'translational lift' and accounts for the fact that a helicopter requires less power to maintain height in forward flight than it does in the hover (Fig. 5.4).

Now remember that a helicopter, unlike a conventional aircraft, does not necessarily have to be pointing in the direction that it is moving and that the pilot must tell the tail where to go at all times. Consider a helicopter which is flying forwards and about to make a turn. First you must use lateral cyclic (aileron) to produce a bank. This applies a sideways lift component which starts the model turning and you must immediately apply tail rotor (rudder) to make the fuselage follow the turn. The result of this is that the rotor *disc* shows a greater angle of incidence relative to the direction in which the model was originally travelling and, therefore, more lift (Fig. 5.5). This means that fore/aft cyclic (elevator) is not required and a turn is made with co-ordinated lateral cyclic and tail rotor (aileron/rudder). If the model is travelling at some speed and/or a sharp turn is made, it will in fact gain height despite the fact that no back cyclic is applied.

Be warned, however, that the story does not end there, since helicopters display markedly different characteristics between right and left turns! Practise the above and familiarise yourself with the co-ordination required for turns in each direction before trying to fly proper circuits. This will reduce the possibility of unpleasant surprises.

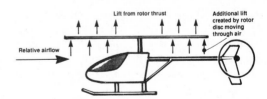

Fig. 5.4 Translational lift.

Fig. 5.5 Lift due to turn.

Hovering close to the ground

Let's go back to the situation where the model is hovering in calm air. Below a height roughly equal to the diameter of the rotor, the model will be very lively and difficult to keep stationary due to interference between the ground and the downwash from the rotors. In essence the model is balanced on a bubble of air and keeps trying to slide off it. Climb a little higher and things become much smoother because you are out of the so-called 'ground effect'.

In flat calm conditions, this effect can be clearly seen, since the exhaust smoke will be observed to be blown away from the model by the rotors when out of ground effect (Fig. 5.6), while it will tend to form a cloud under the helicopter, or even 'leak' up through the middle of the rotors, when in ground effect (Fig. 5.7).

If we now add a breeze to this situation, the bubble of air tends to be blown away from under the model and the effect occurs at a lower altitude (Fig. 5.8). In a strong enough wind the ground effect is virtually non-existent.

Another aspect of the calm air hover is that the tail has to be 'flown', or positioned, all the time, whereas a wind produces a 'weathercock' effect which makes things much easier. However, this weathercock effect influences the torque/tail rotor balance and results in a change of tail rotor trim.

Remember that the primary purpose of the tail rotor is to counteract the torque effect of the main rotor and maintain the fuselage at a constant heading. If we add our weathercock effect on to this, the tail rotor is now too effective and a trim change is required (Fig. 5.9). This trim change will vary with wind strength. On a model with clockwise rotating rotors (viewed from above) this will mean more left trim as the wind

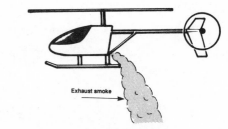

Fig. 5.6 Out of ground effect.

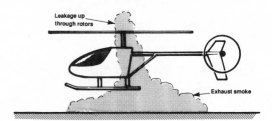

Fig. 5.7 In ground effect.

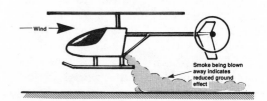

Fig. 5.8 Effect of wind on ground effect.

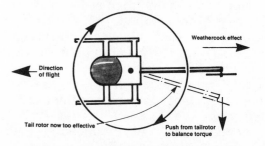

Fig. 5.9 Tail rotor trim change in wind.

becomes stronger. Anticlockwise rotation means more right trim is required.

All of this means that hovering in a wind is rather easier, since the ground effect is less marked and the tail is easier to control, despite a small trim change. Exactly the same situation applies when the model is flying forwards in calm, or windy, air.

One other aspect of hovering in a wind is that it will tend to mask any offset in the tail rotor trim. This offset will be easily detectable in calm air since the helicopter will turn slowly round. In a wind, however, the model will only turn until the trim offset is balanced by the weathercock effect. It will then maintain a constant heading at an angle *to the wind*. This effect is best corrected by observing the exhaust smoke and trimming the model so that the tail boom is pointing in the same direction that the smoke is being blown. If a gyro is fitted, this can tend to hide the effect of the trim offset and can, in gusty conditions, cause the tail to oscillate and lead to the mistaken conclusion that the gyro is too sensitive.

Other trim changes

Another, less known, effect of the tail rotor is that it requires a lateral cyclic trim offset to compensate for the sideways push which it applies (Fig. 5.10). If we consider a machine with clockwise blade rotation, the tail rotor has to apply a push to the right side of the tail to cancel the torque reaction. Apart from preventing the helicopter from rotating about its vertical axis, this also makes the model drift to its left and requires some right cyclic trim to balance it. This trim offset is virtually constant and is not very dependent on forward speed.

When performing the previously described 'tail-in circle', this effect can be quite noticeable and, for contest work, it is normal to turn in the opposite direction to mask it. A model with a clockwise rotor will already have a slight lean to the right and a turn in that direction will require a greater – and more noticeable – bank than a turn to the left.

In theory, some lateral trim should also be required when hovering in a wind, or flying forwards, to cancel out

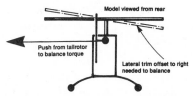

Fig. 5.10 Lateral trim offset due to tail rotor.

the additional lift produced by the forward travelling blade. In my experience, however, this effect is negligible. It would, perhaps, be significant on machines with low rotor speeds and is just noticeable when hovering tail to wind, which requires opposite trim offset.

Increasing speed

Flying forwards is exactly the same as hovering in a wind except that you now have conciously to do things which you probably did automatically in the hover. First of all, some forward cyclic is needed to initiate the forward movement. Note that the word used was *initiate*, not *perpetuate*. If you held on the forward stick, the nose down attitude would increase and the model would move away from you at ever increasing speed and things would rapidly develop into an uncontrollable situation for the novice.

Forward cyclic is applied only long enough to produce a slight nose down attitude in the model. The fore/aft cyclic is then returned to neutral and the machine will accelerate up to a speed consistent with that attitude and stay there. For initial attempts it is best to apply only very short 'stabs' of cyclic control. If you practised walking around with the model in the hover, you should have got the hang of this already. What you should try to remember is that a helicopter is essentially a frictionless device and, once moving, will tend to continue moving until an opposite command is given to stop it. From this it follows that, if a given command is held on, the result is a steadily increasing speed.

Once the machine starts to move, there will be a loss of lift due to the sideways component being used to produce the movement and more power will be required. However, this effect is only temporary since, once moving, the already described translational lift will produce a gain in altitude unless power is reduced.

Now that the machine is moving (remember – not too fast at first), you should notice the change in tail rotor trim. Face up to the fact *now* that you simply cannot keep altering the trim to suit every speed or situation that you may encounter. You must learn to 'fly the tail' all the time by using the rudder stick. After all, you are using *proportional* radio gear are you not? Make the dog wag the tail rather than the other way round. Eventually you will reach the point where you will wonder why one thumb appears to be getting tired and will look down to find that you were holding on a lot of stick trim without even being aware of it!

This trim change will be very noticeable on early, fixed pitch machines, less noticeable on collective models and almost non-existent on the latest collective designs. Modern fixed pitch helicopters suffer from trim changes to a lesser degree. Some early designs incorporated fin offset in an attempt to combat it, with varying success.

At this stage it might be a good idea to consider ways of stopping the beast!

It goes slower, sideways

No, I have not switched to a lecture on rally driving, your helicopter is moving forwards and you want to stop it. Easy,

you say, apply back cyclic. Well, yes, it can be that easy if you are only moving fairly slowly, but bear in mind that to stop in a reasonable distance you have to hold on the control long enough to raise the nose and apply a braking force. When the machine stops, you must immediately lower the nose and increase the power to the hover level. If the model is travelling at some speed, things become much more complicated. Raising the nose will cause an increase in translational lift and make the helicopter climb – possibly quite sharply. To avoid this you must *reduce* power yet be ready to level out and *increase* power when the motion stops – not easy for the novice.

Fortunately, there is an easier, if rather untidy, way which you have already learned if you did the figure eights across wind which were suggested earlier. Simply apply lateral cyclic and tail rotor commands to bank and turn the model so that it presents its side view to the direction of travel. The resulting sharp increase in drag will provide a rapid deceleration and far less sideways cyclic will be required to provide braking effort. If you overdo it, the model will merely slip sideways, which is much easier to control than a tail down reversal into the ground. You may by now have learned that this is probably the most expensive way to crash!

Close-up of the *Kalt/Heim* 'Longranger'.

To sum up all of the above in one phrase – cyclic controls speed, throttle controls height.

That first circuit

Now, at last, we come to your first true circuit. There are two ways of flying a circuit with a helicopter (at least!). The first is what might be termed the 'fixed wing' approach. By this I mean large fast circuits similar to those flown by a conventional aircraft. Second, is the slow, close in, type of circuit which is much more characteristic of a helicopter and which is more accurately described as a 'hovering manoeuvre'.

Graduates from fixed wing models will find the first type the most natural way to go, but they can become dangerous if you get into trouble or become disorientated. In this situation you will automatically revert to those fixed-wing reflexes which you spent so much time in developing and they can lead you sadly astray! Nonetheless, this is probably the best way to go for that first circuit whether or not you have any previous model flying experience.

If you used floats on your model during the initial learning period and have since removed them, it would be well worth replacing them for your first circuits. For one thing, they will limit the forward speed which can be developed. They will also aid orientation and allow the model to be landed safely while still moving (in *any* direction!) which is not true of a model equipped with skids. If you find yourself in the position of having to land the model some distance away (which you will), here again they will be of great help.

Right, we can't delay it any longer. Starting from a stable hover, push in some forward cyclic and add some throttle. Don't bother to reduce power

as the model accelerates, let it climb. You will notice that the model tends to yaw to the right (on clockwise rotors) and fly crabwise. When you become more proficient, you may want to re-trim; at this stage correct it with the stick, or just let it crab, since this will help to reduce problems during the more difficult slowing down phase.

Having travelled a reasonable distance into wind (you *did* wait three years for a day with a light breeze didn't you?), apply some sideways cyclic to bank the model and start a turn. Avoid any tendency to pull the model round with back cyclic – this should not be necessary and will rob you of forward speed which is not advisable at this stage. What *will* be necessary, however, is to use the tail rotor in the direction of the turn to keep the fuselage pointing in the direction of travel.

A common fault here is to think of the rotor disc as being the model, and watch it describe a graceful turn only to find that the fuselage is now pointing its tail at the ground. At this point, you will either slide backwards into the ground (no, the model, stupid) or execute a neat stall turn and dig a hole with the nose! Now you know why I advised you to let it climb.

This situation is complicated by the fact that the majority of models have clockwise rotating rotors and most pilots are right handed. By a quirk of human nature most right-handed pilots want to turn left (it's all in the mind), while your clockwise-rotating, forward-flying helicopter is still stubbornly trying to yaw to the right (Fig. 5.11). QED. You could, of course, defy convention and make all your early turns to the right. What this all boils down to is that, if you make a turn to the left while flying forwards at high speed with clockwise blade rotation, you will probably need to apply full left tail rotor. Some models are

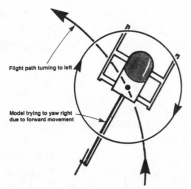

Flight path turning to left

Model trying to yaw right
due to forward movement

Fig. 5.11 Right yaw due to clockwise rotor.

worse than others in this respect due to variations in fin area, tail rotor disc area and about 573 other variables.

Assuming that you manage to complete your first 180° turn and are now starting a down wind leg, use lateral cyclic to roll the model back to level flight. Remember that you need to hold some tail rotor on to fly straight. If you forget, the helicopter will resume flying crabwise and give you a fairly gentle reminder.

I do not intend, now or ever, to become involved in any controversy about downwind turns, *but* when making downwind turns with a helicopter you should ensure that your *groundspeed* downwind is faster than the wind speed (Fig. 5.12). You can easily get into a situation where the model is flying forwards relative to the *ground* but is actually flying backwards *through the air*. This is an unstable condition and the model will attempt to turn through 180° to face the direction of the airflow. The effect to the pilot is that the model has just made a half turn and proceeded to fly backwards (Fig. 5.13). While you are confused, why not prepare yourself for a chat with your bank manager?

If in doubt

This is a good time to consider what you should do in this kind of emergency. If you are in any way doubtful about what is happening, or are disorientated or confused, the first rule of model helicopter flying is to add power and *go up*. Believe it or not, height is not dangerous to this type of model! I have seen choppers almost totally destroyed from a height of less than three inches, yet have seen many crashes which started at 100 feet, or more, and produced only minimal damage. Don't be afraid of altitude or power, it buys you a very useful commodity – time.

If the model is rotating, or *apparently* flying backwards, or you are in *any* doubt about what it is doing, apply some forward cyclic. This should make the model start to move in the direction which it is pointing or stop the rotation. Attempting to stop the rotation directly may make matters worse, since you may well push the rudder stick the wrong way. If the rotation is due to something having broken on the model, you have another problem which we will discuss in a later chapter. Now, back to the circuit.

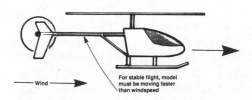

Wind

For stable flight, model
must be moving faster
than windspeed

Fig. 5.12 Keep groundspeed higher than airspeed.

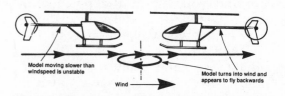

Model moving slower than
windspeed is unstable

Wind

Model turns into wind and
appears to fly backwards

Fig. 5.13 Effect of insufficient airspeed downwind.

Having completed your downwind leg, you now make another turn to bring the model back into wind. This introduces another danger (you guessed!) if your airspeed after the turn is not higher than the wind speed. The model may now be facing you and flying forwards through the air yet be stationary, or flying backwards, relative to the ground. You are not ready for the nose-in hover at this stage, so some other remedy is required.

My solution to this problem during early circuits was deliberately to make a steep slipping turn into wind to ensure a high airspeed (Fig. 5.14). A slight reduction of power before starting the turn helps to produce a higher rate of descent. This can develop into a bad habit later, so you should work away at producing a more controlled turn and slow steady flight into wind.

Don't overdo it

So, the model is now flying back towards you, into wind, and you have to bring it down, slow it down and get back into the hover position. Reduce power enough to ensure a rate of descent which will bring the model down to ground level just in front of you. If too great a reduction is required, go round again and start the descent further away (careful!), or lower. This part is much easier if the model is equipped with an autorotation freewheel, but that, too, I will cover later.

As the model approaches the ground, start applying back cyclic to produce a flare, *without adding power*. Do not add power, or release the back stick, until the model stops moving forwards. If in doubt, add power and forward stick and go round again. If you get it right, the model will maintain constant height, with reducing airspeed and increasingly

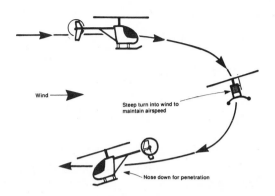

Wind →

Steep turn into wind to maintain airspeed

Nose down for penetration

Fig. 5.14 Steep turn into wind to maintain speed.

nose high attitude until it stops. Push the nose down, add hover power and there you are (Fig. 5.15). Assuming that you have plenty of fuel left, immediately increase power and do another circuit to gain confidence and prove to yourself that it was no fluke. This confidence building will become increasingly important from now on.

Negative pitch helps

The descent from high speed forward flight is an aspect of helicopter flying which many flyers find very difficult. There are several ways in which the process can be made both easier and safer.

So far, the model has been set up in such a way that the pitch of the main blades is always positive. Things can now be made very much easier by the introduction of some negative pitch. Until now, we have avoided this to reduce the risk of the blades striking the boom during the process of learning to hover. When you have reached the stage of flying circuits this risk should have disappeared, due to your being able to perform gentle landings and exercise the necessary throttle control.

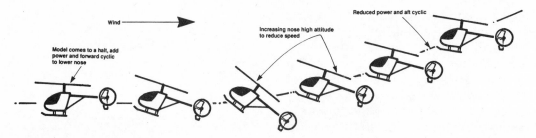

Fig. 5.15 Flare and return to hover.

By now arranging things so that the blades go down to $-1\frac{1}{2}°$ to $-2°$ when the throttle is fully closed, a landing approach can be made with the blades at zero, or slightly negative pitch, but still at a moderate throttle setting to give full control.

Another way of achieving this situation is by use of the 'idle up' switch on your transmitter. This function is more fully described elsewhere but the idea is to raise artificially the idle speed when the throttle stick is pulled right back.

If the model is equipped with an autorotation freewheel, this may be used in conjunction with negative pitch to allow very steep descents to be made with the throttle fully closed. This is more fully discussed in Chapter 8.

Bad habits

When you begin to fly your model in circuits regularly, do be sure to practice both right and left hand circuits to avoid building up a bias towards one particular direction. I have already mentioned that right-handed pilots seem to have a natural tendency to turn left. It is very easy to get into the habit of making *all* of your turns to the left and a point will be reached where you will be very reluctant to turn right. When you do reach this point, the fact that most model helicopters have different handling characteristics between right and left hand turns will make matters even worse.

It cannot be repeated too often – don't develop a bias towards one particular attitude or direction. When you realise that this may be happening, do something about it – immediately!

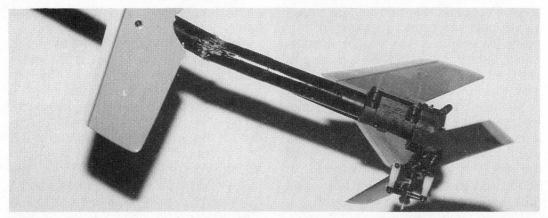

Typical damage caused by a boom strike. Model shown is a *Kalt* 'Cyclone', which has a belt-driven tail rotor. The belt tension tends to increase the boom damage but makes for easier repairs.

Chapter 6
Advanced circuits

Which way is it going?

HAVING REACHED the point of flying your model around in circuits, rather like a fixed-wing model, you will sooner or later – probably sooner – arrive at a point where you are unsure of the model's exact position or attitude. There are many variations on this situation, ranging from a momentary doubt all the way up to total disorientation followed by loss of control and a crash.

The model helicopter pilot is not alone in suffering from this problem. Fixed-wing model flyers have to go through this same situation during the learning stages. However, whereas a conventional model will tend to go on flying, the model helicopter needs to be *flown* all the time and the risk of a crash due to disorientation is much greater.

Curiously enough, the problem does not relate to the quality of the pilot's eyesight. It does not matter how well you may be able to *see* the model if you are unable to relate the information in

There is a tendency among helicopter flyers to use standardised, commercially-available trim on their models. This *Heim* 'Lockheed', by Jim Fox, is a notable exception!

terms of the action required. For this reason, it is undoubtedly true that the problem becomes less as you become more experienced and will eventually disappear. This is small comfort to those who are currently crashing models due to becoming disorientated, so let's see what can be done to help matters.

1. Make more of the model visible. I have found it to be a great help if the main rotor blades are covered with a glossy white material. In sunlight the rotor *disc* becomes visible and this gives more information on the roll attitude of the model. A model helicopter is a very narrow object and, unless the disc can be seen, the only indication on whether the model is banked or level comes from observation of the undercarriage skids. Fig. 6.1 indicates the type of situation we are considering. Fig. 6.2 shows the effect of making the disc visible. In poor light, the effect is much less marked but there is still more of the disc visible, particularly if the model is against some background other than the sky.

2. The above two illustrations also indicate the difficulty which can be experienced in discerning whether the model is coming towards you or going away. This is a more difficult problem to solve but, assuming that the model is a pod and boom type, one solution is to paint the nose cowling a highly visible colour. Many people see one particular colour far better than others and, if this is so in your case, this is the colour to paint your pod. With this type, the remainder of the model is usually predominantly black, which means that if you can see lots of colour it must be coming towards you!

3. Model shape can be a help too. Some designs (notably the *Hirobo* range) feature a horizontal stabiliser with

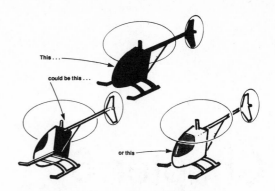

Fig. 6.1 Disorientation in silhouette.

Fig. 6.2 Silhouette plus disc.

twin fins (Fig. 6.3). This can help to give both roll and direction information, particularly if the fins are painted different colours on the inner and outer faces.

4. When you have enough experience to have reached the stage where crashes are a rare occurrence (if ever!), the greatest aid to orientation is to fit a scale type fuselage to your model. This is invariably wider and deeper, which is a great help. The greater cost and effort involved in repairing it probably helps to reduce the risks taken too!

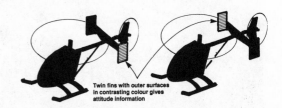

Fig. 6.3 Tailplane with twin fins.

Maximum speed

When you are competent at flying your model around like a fixed-wing aircraft, you will find that you are using more and more power until you reach a point where the throttle is fully open. The model is now flying at the maximum speed of which it is capable and is in a situation where all power above that required to maintain height goes into making the model move forwards. This means that the model will be in a marked nose down attitude (Fig. 6.4).

In this situation, several of the trim balances – and compromises – are considerably changed. Tail rotor trim certainly becomes very complex under these conditions. We have already seen that the weathercock effect due to forward flight makes the tail rotor too effective. This is further complicated if a helicopter radio with some form of collective/tail rotor mixing is used, since this will *increase* the tail rotor pitch to compensate for the increased power and pitch being used.

For this reason, helicopter radios which incorporate a second idle-up setting ('idle up 2') will usually have some means of modifying the tail rotor response when this feature is selected. This is achieved by switching in a new set of 'up' and 'down' compensation adjustments (*JR* sets), or adding a control to reduce the amount of 'up' compensation (*Futaba* sets). Another method is simply to switch off the tail compensation system and some radios are fitted with an easily accessible switch for this purpose.

At high speeds the fore/aft cyclic response becomes very critical in some designs. In my opinion, there is a definite relationship between the size and incidence angle of the horizontal stabiliser (tailplane) and the angle of the mainshaft (some designs have the shaft

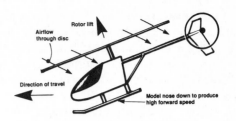

Fig. 6.4 High speed forward flight.

raked forwards). However, this relationship has not so far been sufficiently investigated to ensure that a given design will be stable in fast forward flight. Not all authorities agree on this point and many experienced flyers maintain that the horizontal stabiliser is unnecessary.

The most common problem experienced is that the model porpoises or is excessively sensitive to elevator input. Another common trait is for the model to pitch up as speed increases, making it difficult, if not impossible, to maintain a shallow dive as an entry to an aerobatic manoeuvre. Any free play or slop in the fore/aft cyclic linkages will aggravate this situation. Some designs are far better than others regarding the linkages associated with this control. Systems which employ two pushrods to the swashplate (one in front and one behind) are the ones to look for.

Rapid descent

With increasing speed, the difficulties associated with descent and tranlation back to hovering flight become more acute. It may be found that the model will not descend at all unless a considerable amount of negative pitch is available.

While you can, of course, slow the model down before beginning a descent, there will still be problems if you fly in windy weather. Even if the model is flying slowly relative to the ground, its *airspeed* may still be quite high. Here again, the more advanced radios cater for this situation by incorporating a separate low pitch adjustment associated with the 'idle up 2' function. By this means, it is possible to have more negative pitch than usual (say -5°) when required.

The whole subject of high speed forward flight will become of increased importance when you attempt to perform aerobatics, as described in Chapter 9.

The *Kyosho* 'Concept' has become very popular, due to its ability to withstand punishment and the ready availability of parts. At the time of writing, however, the ideal design of the main rotor blade was still to be established.

Chapter 7
Advanced hovering

Hovering circuits

A NY MANOEUVRE, or circuit, which your model may perform while travelling fairly slowly may be considered as an advanced hovering manoeuvre. Here the model is not subject, to any significant degree, to the trim changes or translational lift effects which occur during fast forward flight.

We have already considered the tail-in circle, which can be performed in either direction. The same manoeuvre can be performed with the model sideways on to you and travelling forwards (Fig. 7.1), or backwards (Fig. 7.2), again in either direction.

So far, we have only considered circles around the pilot. The next step is to perform a circle, or circuit, off to one side (Fig. 7.3). This is something which many flyers find to be extremely difficult and here, as before, the longer you delay the potentially more difficult it becomes. There is no easy solution to this one, other than doing the first ones at a safe altitude, which means at some speed since it is difficult to fly slowly at any height or distance.

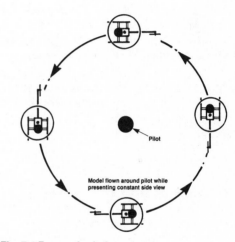

Fig. 7.1 Forwards circle.

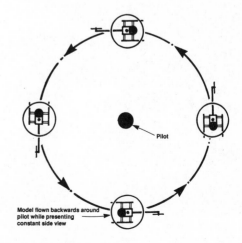

Fig. 7.2 Backwards circle.

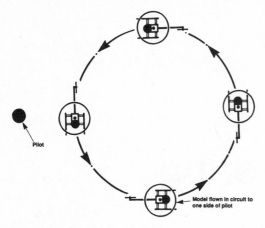

Fig. 7.3 Circle with pilot outside.

From this point you can progressively reduce both the height and the speed until the model is performing very slow circles just above the ground. However, this can take a very long time to accomplish – some flyers never manage it – and will bring you closer and closer to the next stage to be conquered – the nose-in hover.

The nose-in hover

Having spent a great deal of time on learning to hover in the 'safe base' position, you will reach a point where your carefully acquired reflexes begin to work against you. When the model is facing you instead of pointing away from you, the fore/aft and lateral cyclic controls will appear to be reversed. It is very difficult to make this transition – here, again, some flyers never do – and there are many, varied ways which have been suggested to help in the initial stages.

If you can fly the model around in circuits, you will have already reached the point where you can fly the model towards you, a situation which will present no problems to experienced fixed-wing flyers. However, when you try to *stop* the model in that position, the whole situation seems to suddenly change and things can rapidly reach a point of total confusion. This is due to the fact that the elevator control on a helicopter works differently between hovering and moving forward. In this situation it seems to be a natural reaction to pull in back cyclic which leads to the model reversing away from you. Remember the cardinal rule in this situation is to push *both sticks forward*, but do be ready to leap out of the way if necessary!

The *GMP* 'Legend' is the first really successful model to feature a so-called 'flybarless' rotor head. Careful design and weighting of the blades has produced a performance which is indistinguishable from most flybar-equipped models – and better than some!

Practise flying the model towards you at slower and slower speed (and at a safe height) with short stops at frequent intervals. Curiously enough, I found that, if this is done in a fairly strong, but steady, wind, it is possible to visualise the model as flying forwards even when it is stationary relative to the ground! Also, in this situation, the elevator control behaves more like it does on a fixed-wing model rather than as it does on a hovering helicopter. It is also easier to stop the forward movement in this situation, since many models require a positive effort to make headway against anything more than a stiff breeze.

Should you get into difficulties during this situation, a better method of recovery is to execute a half turn with the tail rotor control and allow the model to head off downwind. It can then be turned back into wind for another attempt.

This is a good time to discuss a little further the differences in elevator response between hovering and flying forward. In forward flight, the application of up elevator (back cyclic) will make the model climb, like an aircraft. When hovering, the same input will make the model start to move backwards. The actual point of this transition depends on several factors and it is this change of response which takes some getting used to, particularly for those with lots of fixed-wing experience.

Another method of learning to hover with the model facing you is to place it on the ground in this attitude and learn to fly again from scratch. This is a very frustrating approach, however, and you will be constantly tempted to turn the model round and get on with some real flying.

The final move is to turn around, taking the model with you, as before, and you will be performing one of the most difficult of all hovering manoeuvres – the nose-in circle.

Pirouettes

In its simplest form, this manoeuvre consists of placing the model in a stable hover and applying full left or right tail rotor command. In theory, the model should rotate about its vertical axis until the control is released and then stop. If the model should decide to rotate on its own accord due to something having broken, it will usually stay in one spot and rotate quite happily. When the same thing is attempted deliberately, however, one turn is usually enough to send the model shooting off at great speed in some totally unexpected direction!

Once again we return to the old advice to practise at a safe height. If rate switches are in use, they should be set in the low position on the cyclic controls, since difficulties are usually pilot-induced (unintentionally) and it helps to make the model as docile as possible. Many models require some lateral cyclic input to assist in making a stable flat turn. This is usually – but not always – in the same direction as the tail rotor command.

If a rudder rate switch is available, this should be set to high rate to encourage the model to turn as rapidly as possible. Although this will exaggerate any effects of yaw/roll coupling, it will make first attempts less traumatic. Losing control and/or orientation of a very slowly turning helicopter is not recommended.

Constant heading circle

You can combine the pirouette with the hovering circuit by turning around and taking the model around too, as before, but with the model always pointing into wind (Fig. 7.4). Thus the model performs a slow pirouette relative to the pilot while turning around the pilot. If you are close to mastering the slow pirouette, you may find this to be easier since the model is always pointing into wind.

Another variation on this is to hover the model at a *constant heading* and walk slowly round it (Fig. 7.5). This manoeuvre is known as a 'pilot's promenade'.

The horizontal eight

This is not to be confused with our old friend the 'lazy eight' (as illustrated in Fig 5.3) described earlier. It is a true figure eight circuit flown at slow speed in front of the pilot (Fig. 7.6) and forms one of the compulsory manoeuvres flown in FAI contests. Most authorities agree that it is possibly the most difficult of all the hovering manoeuvres, and it combines the difficulties of both the nose-in hover and the pirouette. In contests it has to be flown over four marker flags which makes it even more difficult.

If you have become fairly proficient at the nose-in hover, you may find that this figure is easier to perform by standing with your back to the wind and taking off and landing in the nose-in position. This makes the figure identical to the 'lazy eight' where the nose of the model does not actually *cross* the pilot's eye line. This is a useful 'cheat' for FAI contests where the actual path of the model is rigidly defined.

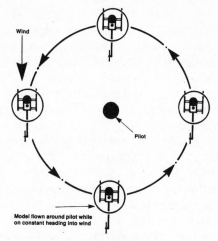

Fig. 7.4 Constant heading circle.

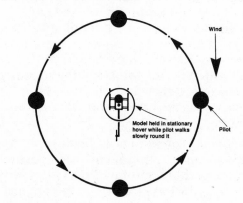

Fig. 7.5 Promenade.

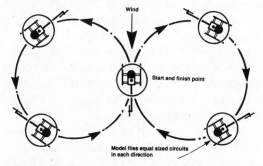

Fig. 7.6 Horizontal eight.

Chapter 8
Autorotation

Pitch

STRICTLY speaking, there are two types of autorotation: as a safety device aimed at landing the model in one piece after an engine failure, or as an aerobatic manoeuvre. The difference is that, in the former, it does not matter *where* the model is landed – as long as the area is clear of people and property – or how untidy the landing is, while, in the latter case, it must look good *and* land on a small spot.

Basically, the autorotation descent is performed by reducing the pitch of the main blades to a negative figure – typically –2° to –3° – so that the blades will continue to rotate while the model is in an engine-off descent. The actual amount of pitch used is quite critical and controls the 'glide' angle. Too much negative will give a very rapid descent with high blade speed, while insufficient negative will give a shallow glide with low rotor RPM. It may be difficult to imagine the concept of a helicopter 'gliding' but this is an accurate description of the process, since it is directly comparable to a gliding fixed-wing model. With a fixed-wing machine the

forward movement is caused by the descent (i.e. elevator controls speed) and care must be taken to keep the airspeed up to avoid stalling. With a helicopter, the rotation is caused by the descent and the blade speed must be maintained to avoid a 'stall' and loss of control.

The analogy can be carried even further if we consider what happens as we approach the stall. With an aircraft, the nose can be raised and the angle of attack increased until the model is flying very slowly but not quite stalling. Similarly we can reduce the negative pitch of the blades – and even go slightly positive – without the blades actually stopping. However this is a dangerous situation since there will be insufficient energy in the system to stop the model and land. From this, we can see that it is possible to control both the rate and angle of descent by varying the pitch (Fig. 8.1). However, this does need lots of practice to get right.

There will be one optimum pitch setting which gives the maximum blade RPM and this is the ideal point to aim for when setting up the model. Note that the word used is 'ideal' rather than 'correct', since the correct pitch may be influenced by other factors. The correct

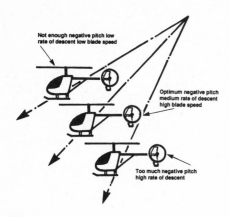

Not enough negative pitch low rate of descent low blade speed

Optimum negative pitch medium rate of descent high blade speed

Too much negative pitch high rate of descent

Fig. 8.1 Effect of pitch on glide angle.

pitch for any model can only be determined by experiment, which is why experienced contest flyers prefer to have too much negative and 'fly the pitch' on the way down. If you are only interested in autorotation as a means of saving the model in the event of an engine failure, the pitch can simply be set to the manufacturer's recommended figure (or, if in doubt, –2½°). However, it must be stressed that you must still practise the manoeuvre if you are to stand *any* chance of success in an emergency situation.

Autorotation freewheels

So far, we have not considered the effect of an autorotation clutch on the model. This device should more accurately be described as a freewheel, the intent of which is to allow the blades to rotate at high speed while the motor is idling or stopped. While this condition will exist anyway as soon as the clutch has disengaged, there are good reasons for allowing the rotor to rotate freely. It takes a measurable time for the motor to decelerate to the point where the clutch disengages and, during this time, it will tend to slow the rotor, which is undesirable. Another reason is that, without such a freewheel, the tail rotor will continue to rotate at a normal speed and attempt to cancel out a torque effect which is no longer present.

This means that, without a freewheel, the result is an unwanted yawing effect which makes the landing more difficult, particularly if tail rotor/collective pitch mixing is being used. This mixing increases the tail rotor pitch to compensate for the increased torque when collective pitch is added, but in an autorotation landing there is no torque

I like to produce models which are a little different from the 'norm'. One example is this *Kalt* 'Longranger' body, fitted with *Heim* mechanics.

at all so the yaw effect is even more pronounced. To combat this, the free-wheel is normally positioned in the main gearwheel which drives the rotor shaft (Fig. 8.2) and the result is that the tail rotor slows with the motor and acually stops when the clutch dis-engages. This does mean, of course, that there is no control over the model's yaw axis (rudder to you fixed-wing flyers) during the descent, although the natural weathercock effect of the fuse-lage will keep it lined up in the direction of flight. Because of this, specialised mo-dels intended for use in FAI contests now usually have the option of continuing to drive the tail so that the model *can* be steered on the way down. This is only really effective if used in conjunction with a special radio outfit which allows the tail rotor pitch to be reduced to zero when the motor is stopped.

One other benefit of fitting the free-wheel in the main gear is that the rotor is not encumbered by the rest of the drive train, including the various reduc-tion gears and tail drive and is allowed to spin much more freely than would otherwise be the case.

The landing

Well now, your helicopter is approach-ing the ground at a great rate of knots with the engine idling and you have to land it – gently. It used to be thought that the correct technique was to add positive pitch at *just* the right moment to give a survivable – if not gentle – landing. On very early model helicopters this was probably the only method which stood any chance of success, but only just! Both then and now, it is a very difficult approach which requires *very* accurate timing.

With modern designs, the correct method is to make the descent with

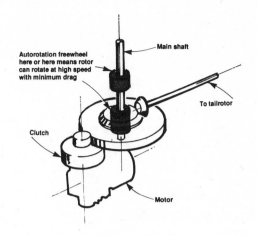

Fig. 8.2 Position of autorotation clutch.

some forward speed and then use this speed to flare like an aircraft, still holding a negative pitch setting (Fig. 8.3). In this way, the model can be brought to a halt a short distance from the ground with all of the blade energy and pitch range still available to make the landing. Even if you make a complete mess of it, the model only has a few inches to fall. The biggest danger is that of applying too much pitch at this point, causing the model to gain height again while dissipating all the useful blade energy. Another effect of the flare is to wind up the blade speed which helps to give a greater safety margin.

In recent times the greater availability of heavy GRP blades has made this manoeuvre much easier and neater. However, these blades do increase the damage which can be done to the model when you get it wrong. They also increase the overall cost of such a mistake.

First attempts should be made by starting from a safe height and closing the throttle fully without stopping the engine – don't use the 'throttle hold' switch at this stage. If the model is set up correctly, it should make a steep descent under full control. You should see the tail rotor slow right down or

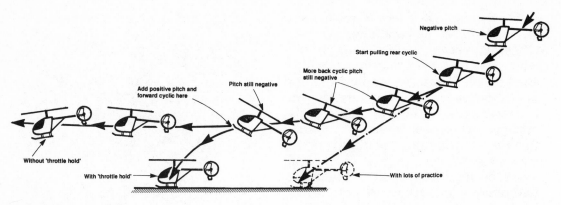

Negative pitch

Start pulling rear cyclic

More back cyclic pitch
still negative

Pitch still negative

Add positive pitch and
forward cyclic here

Without 'throttle hold'

With 'throttle hold'

With lots of practice

Fig. 8.3 Autorotation flare.

even stop. While it is still at a safe height, apply back cyclic to flare the model into level flight and simultaneously add power to return to the hover position. Practise this until you can bring the model to a stop, in the hover, a few inches from the ground and just in front of you. If you are a fixed-wing flyer, this part should be fairly easy!

Now comes the most difficult part – do it again but with the 'throttle hold' switched on as the model starts to descend. If the 'hold' is set to give a safe idle, there should still be plenty of time to switch it off and recover even if you make a complete mess of things. The difficulty lies in convincing yourself of that! If all is well, it will be simply a matter of lowering the model gently to the ground from the low level hover position. It really is that simple since you have already conquered the difficult part – the descent and flare.

It can be quite difficult to find the nerve (it can be quite difficult to find the switch too) to do your first 'full-down autorotation' (a descriptive American term). Some models will drop very rapidly during the early part of the descent while the main rotor winds up to a suitable speed. A trick used in FAI contests is to use the 'idle up' switch to give a high blade RPM as the throttle is closed. Using this technique, it is

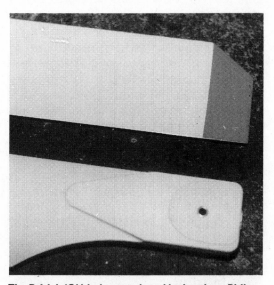

The British 'G' blades, produced by brothers Phil and Dave George, have done much to bring quality GRP blades within the reach of the average modeller.

possible to perform a safe autorotation from a very low level.

One point to watch is that of practising the 'power up' recovery described above too often, until the actual performance of a real power off landing becomes a real hurdle. At this point, your chances of success are actually considerably reduced, since a power on recovery requires a different technique to a power off landing – and you have been practising the wrong thing!

Not too low!

Having convinced yourself that you can safely find the 'hold' switch and abort an autorotation landing, you should beware of making a habit of this. When the model is at some height and still moving forwards it will present no problems. However, if performed very late – and low, there may be insufficient forward speed to stabilise the tail and the result of a sudden power application will be to make the model swing round. If you have been 'holding off' while making your mind up, the blade speed may have decayed to a very low level which will make things even worse. If in doubt, land it anyway – it may do less damage!

Even with a perfectly judged autorotation, there may still be some tendency for the model to swing round in the same direction as the blade rotation. This will normally not be apparent until just before the point of touchdown. There can be several reasons for this. If the clutch is not fully disengaging and the tail rotor is still turning, this will produce a sideways push to the tail. This will be made worse if some tail compensation is in use, as already described. The cure is to improve the clutch operation or use one of the new radios which allow you to 'feather' the tail rotor when the 'hold' switch is operated. Also, as the model's forward speed drops to zero and the pitch is increased for landing, there is a large drag on the lower mainshaft bearing which can produce a yaw effect. It is essential that this bearing is as free as possible. Many models now incorporate a thrust race below this bearing to reduce this effect.

If the swing around on landing is severe, it may be due to using too much pitch, which will aggravate the above problems. Many authorities state that

Wooden blades can be used in weighted or unweighted form and can be neatly finished off by covering with heatshrink sleeving (below).

American *Yale* 'Truespin' blades.

you should use 10°–12° or more pitch for autorotations. I have found 8°–9° to be perfectly adequate and suggest that, if you need more than this, there is something wrong.

Circuits

With lots of practice and increasing confidence, it is possible to steer the model around the sky quite a lot during an autorotation. By banking the model and using back cyclic, the model can be turned rather like a fixed-wing model. The tail will 'weathercock' and keep the nose pointing in the direction that the model is travelling. Here again, the use of heavy GRP blades and a 'driven tail' make this much easier and safer.

When attempting to land on a small spot, you may indeed find it easier to start your autorotation with the model heading away from you in a downwind direction and perform a 180° turn during the descent. This can make it easier to arrive at the correct spot by varying the radius and steepness of the turn.

To return to an earlier point, while an autorotation landing can be used as a method of safely landing a model which has a dead engine, or some other problem, it does need *practice*. So, even if you don't intend to compete in FAI contests where it is necessary to perform smooth, polished, engine-off landings in a small box, why not have a go at doing some untidy, but gentle, ones somewhere in the same field?

Finally, if the model is *low and slow* and you think you have made a mess of things, remember that 'chickening out' and switching off the 'hold' will probably just produce a more expensive crash!

The *GMP* 'Legend' at an all-up weight of around 9 lb. With a 0.61 engine, gives superb engine-on performance. Engine-off performance – or autorotation – is exceptional.

Chapter 9
Aerobatics

Radio requirements

WHEN YOU decide that you wish to try flying aerobatics with your helicopter, you should give serious thought to the degree of commitment that you are willing to make to your sport/hobby. While not absolutely essential, a helicopter radio will make things much easier – which probably means *less* expensive in the long run!

If you are still using a standard radio system and only wish to execute the occasional loop or roll, then you can continue with your existing equipment, but you should realise that you are not going to be able to perform *round* loops or *axial* rolls. Even the best aerobatic helicopter/pilot combination available will not be able to perform these manoeuvres without some help from purpose-designed radio equipment.

Assuming that you decide that you wish to take things seriously and intend to acquire suitable equipment, you should look for a helicopter radio which has *two* idle-up systems, plus a throttle hold switch, with separate collective pitch adjustments on each. These will be used to set things up for three separate flight conditions:

1. Hovering manoeuvres – Idle up 1.
2. Aerobatic manoeuvres – Idle up 2.
3. Autorotation – Throttle hold.

Idle up 1

This should be used to adjust the model in a manner similar to that which you have been used to so far. However, as you now have another set-up available for aerobatics the model can be made less sensitive. Normally, the rate switches will be set in the 'low' position and, if variable gyro sensitivity is available, this will be set in the 'high' position. Only a small amount of negative pitch will be used.

The object here is to make the model fly as smoothly as possible and, ideally, the control movements should be set to the absolute minimum, while the gyro gain should be as high as possible. As the main object is to obtain a smooth hover, the actual idle-up controls should be set to give as nearly as possible a constant engine speed.

Remember that switching off both idle-up functions will give you normal throttle control for starting. It is *essential* that you check that this has been done before attempting to start the engine, otherwise a nasty accident could result.

Idle up 2

All of the settings used here have to be established in flight and most will be the result of some compromise or other. Rate switches will normally be set to the 'high' position, with the gyro sensitivity on the 'low' setting. The amount of negative pitch needed may, in extreme cases, be as much as the amount of positive pitch available (see later).

Control throws need to be sufficient to perform the manoeuvres required – which, with some models, means as much as possible. However, do try to avoid using too much movement as this will make the model 'twitchy' and cause excessive speed loss during manoeuvres.

Gyro gain depends on the individual flyer. The gyro could be dispensed with when the model is in fast forward flight and can, if too powerful, actually hinder the performance of some manoeuvres. Most flyers prefer to retain some gyro

effect but this will normally be a lower value than in the purely hovering mode.

Throttle should be set so that normal hovering RPM is maintained when the throttle/pitch stick is pulled right back to give full negative pitch.

Throttle hold

As previously explained, this will put the throttle servo into a preset position while still allowing the pitch to be controlled by the throttle stick. For autorotation practice, the throttle will be set to give a safe idle speed. In contest flying, the motor must be stopped and the throttle servo will be set to a position which achieves this. One or two helicopter radios are equipped with a second throttle hold option to allow the practice setting to be retained. Some also have a facility which automatically operates the 'hold' facility when the throttle stick is lowered beyond a certain point.

Pitch will be set to a negative figure which is suitable for an autorotation descent. Normally, any limiting adjustment which may have been made to the amount of positive pitch available will

The 'Longranger'. Tuned pipe/silencer installation was a tight squeeze, but the project was well worth the effort. All-up weight is only 10 lb. For a model which is large enough to present transport difficulties in a medium-sized car.

be overridden by this control. This ensures that the maximum amount of pitch is available for landing.

If you are only interested in performing aerobatics on a casual basis and don't want to make the investment involved in one of the more advanced helicopter radios, then one of the more generally available – and cheaper – sets with only one idle-up switch can be used. Here the idle-up facility will be used to set the model up for aerobatics and the normal throttle action used for general flying.

Preparation

As with all the stages so far discussed, during the process of learning to fly aerobatics the model will be put into many very unfamiliar positions and attitudes, so it is essential that your flying capabilities are such that you are not still finding yourself in a position where you are disorientated. Are you still finding yourself in a condition where the model is sitting quite happily in the hover some distance away, but you are reluctant to apply some control input for fear of doing the wrong thing? If so, this is the exact thing that you must work at until you are happy that you can cope.

One thing which will cause problems in attempting any aerobatics is an underpowered helicopter. With aircraft you can start at considerable height and dive to gain speed. An underpowered helicopter will rapidly decelerate as soon as you apply any control input and the model will come to a dead stop – probably inverted. Now is the time to replace that tired old engine and, while you are at it, give the model a *thorough* check over too.

Loops

To most people aerobatics means 'looping the loop' and this is where we shall begin with our helicopter aerobatics. Just about every collective pitch helicopter available should be capable of performing this manoeuvre, but some are more capable than others. If you have any doubts about your particular model, then you should consult the manufacturers, importers, specialist shop, or local expert for advice on the subject.

Assuming that you are happy with your ability to cope with a helicopter in an unfamiliar attitude and with the mechanical soundness of your model, all you really need to do is to get the model up to a safe height, build up lots of forward speed, pull the cyclic stick back and watch it go round. It will probably be very untidy (and you may need that ability to cope with unfamiliar attitudes) but you should not be concerned at this stage with what it looks like, only what it does.

Helicopters differ widely in their reaction to high forward speed. Some become more responsive with increasing speed, others less responsive. This does not only vary from make to make but between individual machines of the same make. I have seen a *Hirobo* '808' which would loop from the hover, while another identical machine would not. Some idea of your particular model's handling characteristics can be gleaned from doing steep stall turns, but eventually you will have to try a proper loop and see what happens. What you should *not* do at this stage is to listen to differing advice on how to do precise *round* loops. Just go ahead and do sloppy, untidy, figure 9's and get used to the idea of throwing your helicopter around.

If you do get into trouble at this stage,

it is likely to take one of three forms:

1. The model does not make it over the top of the loop and starts to fall inverted. This is why you started at a safe height. Hang on to the back stick and full power and the model should right itself.
2. After completing three quarters of a loop the model is reluctant to pull out of the ensuing dive. Here again, just hang on.
3. When the loop is complete the model zooms wildly or comes to a stop in a nose high attitude. Be ready to push the stick forward as the model returns to level flight. You will probably need this anyway to re-establish forward flight. In this situation, some models will run out of RPM and the blades may slow down and the motor begin to labour. Be ready to reduce pitch in order to maintain RPM and controllability.

When you are quite happy and confident with your untidy loops you can start to clean them up a little. This is where the 'idle up' switch on your transmitter starts to become very useful.

Now, once again at a safe height and with lots of forward speed, pull the stick back and, as the model passes through the vertical climb position, reduce the pitch to zero. Keep the pitch at zero around the top half of the loop and then apply positive pitch as the model passes through the vertical dive position. By varying the back stick and the pitch you should eventually be able to achieve a true round loop. You will probably find it

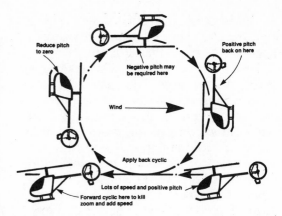

Fig. 9.1 Loop.

necessary to apply some negative pitch at the top of the loop to do this (Fig. 9.1).

Remember – get it round the loop first, *then* tidy it up later.

Rolls

There is something rather incongruous about a helicopter performing a roll, yet, given a suitable model, it is probably easier to do than a loop. With some models, it is easier to produce a reasonable looking roll than it is to perform a truly round loop.

As with the loop, your first roll should be performed by climbing to a safe height, putting on lots of forward speed (it helps to do it downwind) and holding the lateral cyclic hard over until the roll is complete. The nose should be raised slightly just before starting the roll, but don't overdo it, since it will lose you too much of that precious forward speed.

Roll direction for best results depends on the model, but usually should be

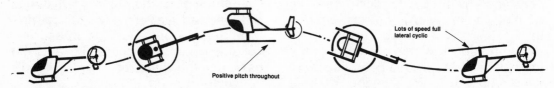

Fig. 9.2 Barrel roll.

away from the forward-going blade. This means rolling to the right with a clockwise main rotor or to the left if the rotor rotates anticlockwise. However, this is not an invariable rule.

Your first attempt will be untidy and probably more like a barrel roll (Fig. 9.2), but don't worry too much about that at this stage. If you get into trouble it will probably take one of the following forms:

1. Roll rate is very slow. If the model only gets as far as being on its side and then starts to fall, apply opposite lateral cyclic to roll out and back stick to recover. Having got as far as the inverted stage, the easiest answer is to pull the stick back and perform a half loop to recover (again, that's why you needed lots of height).

2. The model reaches the inverted point and stops rolling. Apply back stick to half loop back to normal flight. Do it again to make sure you did not just let go of the stick in fright!

3. All forward speed is lost before the roll is complete. Most models will probably complete the roll anyway, but some may begin to fall inverted, in which case use full back stick and pray! The answer to this one is more forward speed which means more power or a cleaner model. *Don't* be tempted to push the stick forward when inverted, as this will kill speed very rapidly. It's much better to add a little up to drop the nose. When you become very proficient, it is possible to coax an underpowered model through a roll, but we will come to that in a moment.

Having mastered the art of performing untidy, diving, barrelly rolls, we can start to improve them. This is where our old friend the 'idle up' switch comes in handy again. Start your roll as before and, as the model approaches the inverted point, pull the throttle stick back to reduce the pitch to zero, or slightly negative. Don't overdo it at this stage. An inverted, climbing helicopter tends to cause the brain and thumbs to go out of synch! As the model rolls from inverted to normal flight, move the throttle stick back to the normal position.

What you are aiming for is something like Fig. 9.3 where the pitch is reduced to around zero when the model is on its side, goes down to negative when inverted, back to zero when the helicopter is on its other side and finally back to normal. Keep practising until you can perform smooth, axial rolls.

There is another approach to the problem of maintaining speed throughout the roll which is used by those of above average ability. Normally, at the entry to the roll, the model is in high speed forward flight which means that it is at full power and in a nose down attitude to prevent it climbing. If this attitude can be maintained throughout the roll, then the model will be continuously pulled forward by the main rotor. In order to keep this nose down attitude during the inverted phase (Fig. 9.4), we need to have as much negative pitch available as the normal positive figure – typically 6°–7°! Obviously, this large pitch range will make the model more difficult to fly in most other situations.

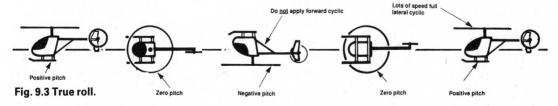

Fig. 9.3 True roll.

Positive pitch

Zero pitch

Do **not** apply forward cyclic

Negative pitch

Zero pitch

Lots of speed full lateral cyclic

Positive pitch

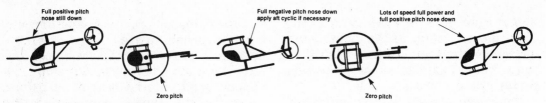

Full positive pitch
nose still down

Full negative pitch nose down
apply aft cyclic if necessary

Lots of speed full power and
full positive pitch nose down

Zero pitch

Zero pitch

Fig. 9.4 Roll with nose down throughout.

Other manoeuvres

Apart from one other ingredient, which I will discuss in a moment, most helicopter aerobatics consist of combinations of the loop and roll. Take for example the reversal, or split ess (Fig. 9.5), consisting of a half roll followed by a half loop. Starting downwind and with lots of speed, roll inverted and hold this for a moment (consult the judges of your particular contest for advice on how long a 'moment' is) with zero, or slight negative pitch. Complete the figure by pulling 'up' and adding positive pitch as the model passes through the vertical dive position. This one is easy to do but difficult to get *right*.

The other ingredient is the humble stall turn, which again is easy to do until you attempt to add lengthy periods of vertical climb or dive as required in contests. Under these conditions the pitch setting becomes very critical. If you simply leave the positive pitch on, the model will fall over backwards during the climb. This situation is made more complicated by the fact that there is no indication from the transmitter stick to tell you exactly where zero pitch is, so you have to fly by feel and observation of the model.

All of the points we have discussed so far can be combined in one manoeuvre, the rolling stall turn (Fig. 9.6), originally known as the Belgian stall turn. This commences with a quarter loop (back cyclic, positive pitch) followed by a vertical climb (neutral cyclic, zero pitch), a half roll (full lateral cyclic), a further

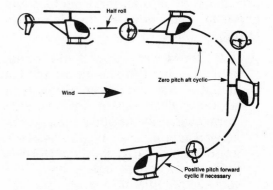

Half roll

Wind

Zero pitch aft cyclic

Positive pitch forward
cyclic if necessary

Fig. 9.5 Split ess.

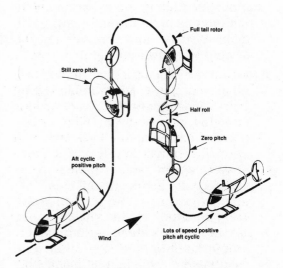

Full tail rotor

Still zero pitch

Half roll

Zero pitch

Aft cyclic
positive pitch

Lots of speed positive
pitch aft cyclic

Wind

Fig. 9.6 Rolling stall turn.

vertical climb (if you are lucky), a stall turn (full rudder), a vertical dive back to the point where you started the climb (still zero pitch) and another quarter loop (back cyclic, positive pitch) to recover. What usually happens is that the model runs out of steam during the half roll, and tumbles backwards. If the model has enough inertia to complete the roll, its eventual path will depend on whether the initial climb was truly vertical and the pitch exactly zero.

The rolling stall turn is one of the most difficult manoeuvres and it should be apparent that it requires a clean, high powered, helicopter. With a suitable model it still requires considerable practice, however, to produce something recognisable. It is only possible to give a general description above on how to go about it, since every helicopter requires its own particular technique to produce the desired result. In particular, it is worth experimenting with the direction of both the roll and the stall turn to see if any improvement can be found.

The problem of sensing just where the actual zero pitch point is on the transmitter can be solved by setting up one of your pitch ranges so that simply pulling the collective stick hard back gives exactly zero pitch. This can also be useful in rolling some models, but may require compromises elsewhere, if you run out of available pitch ranges.

Size comparison with Helimax/'Jetranger' shows how long the 'Longranger' is!

Chapter 10
Advanced aerobatics

Inverted flight

APART FROM a few dedicated individuals who preferred to do it the 'hard way' (we'll discuss that in a moment), the flying of a model helicopter upside down became possible with the introduction of the 'invert switch'. This reversed the action of the pitch, elevator and tail rotor channels so that the model handled in exactly the same manner inverted as it did the normal way up.

For a while after this 'technological leap' everyone was flying their helicopters inverted. The novelty soon wore off, however. Nowadays it is regarded very much as a 'party trick' and there are only a few helicopter radios which feature an 'invert' switch.

Assuming that you wish to become one of the select few and possess a suitable radio, you should set up the collective pitch travel in a manner which gives a mirror image of the normal travel when the invert switch is operated. If the normal travel is, say −3° to +7°, then the invert travel should be +3° to −7° (Fig. 10.1).

Now all you have to do is to take the model up to a safe height, roll it inverted and flip the switch. Your model will now behave in a perfectly normal manner, but the other way up. Orientation can be a problem, however, so take it easy at first. In practice, the model tends to be more stable inverted, since the rotor downwash is not corrupted by the drag of the fuselage.

Contrary to popular belief, both the

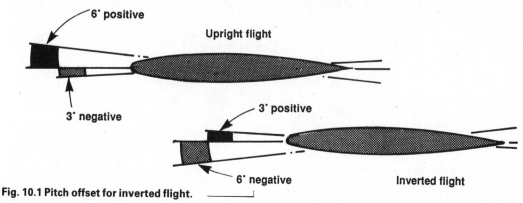

6° positive

Upright flight

3° negative

3° positive

6° negative

Inverted flight

Fig. 10.1 Pitch offset for inverted flight.

tail compensation system and the gyro will work quite normally in this position and the pitch requirement is an exact mirror image of that required for normal flying. The most difficult part of the exercise for fixed-wing flyers lies in convincing yourself that the controls really *do* work normally.

In fact, it is quite possible to fly your model inverted without the use of an invert switch. If a lot of negative pitch is available, as previously described for aerobatics, the model may be rolled inverted and the throttle stick pulled hard back. Do it, as always, at a safe height and remember that the tail was the most difficult function to control initially and is the most likely one to give you problems when the action is the opposite of what you have come to expect. An inverted, pirouetting heli-copter can make even the most hardened flyer turn into a quivering jelly!

This method is becoming increasingly popular and has great benefits in terms of aerobatic flying.

Outside loops

Let's say, straight away, that these are not for the faint hearted, or the poorly-maintained helicopter. Nonetheless, they *are* possible, as several flyers have proved. Obviously you will need lots of negative pitch!

Entry speed is a problem here. Too much speed will certainly be a hindrance to most – but not all – models. Start with the model travelling down-wind and as high as possible. Push the

An example of the very best in scale modelling is this *Bell* 'Huey', produced by Len Mount. The model has full interior detail and all doors and hatches open. Power is provided by a *Super-Tigre* 0.75, which is adequate for the 18 lb model.

collective stick full forward and, as the model passes through the vertical dive position, apply full negative pitch (Fig. 10.2). If the model is reluctant to pull out into inverted flight, the best answer is to roll out and apply back cyclic and positive pitch to recover. The model *should* make it through the inverted position, but will lose lots of speed in the process which can cause any number of effects during the inverted climb phase.

The best course of action here depends on just when the model actually stops:

1. During the initial stages of the climb, the best solution is to apply back cyclic to drop the nose and then roll out.
2. At the vertical climb position, apply full rudder to produce a stall turn and recover by a quarter loop into normal flight.

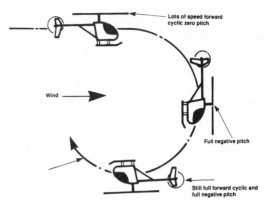

Fig. 10.2 Outside loops.

3. If the model makes it past the vertical climb, hang on to the full forward cyclic and apply full *positive* pitch.

Consecutive manoeuvres

If you have a model which will per-

Additional equipment includes rockets which actually fire, and working lights.

form round loops and axial rolls then it is quite capable of performing several loops or rolls consecutively. The limiting factor here is *your* ability to *fly* the model (a better word might be 'coax') through the manoeuvres without losing too much speed. This ability can only be acquired by constant practice and you *will* damage models in the process. However, one thing that is certain to hold you back in the learning process is a fear of breaking the model and you must conquer this or try something else. This explains why most of today's top helicopter pilots are connected with the model trade in some way!

Now it's up to you

Only a few years ago it was a considerable achievement to fly a model helicopter at all. To be able to fly one around in a circuit made you one of the top flyers in the world. A loop was thought to be possible and there were those who claimed to have seen one.

The modern model helicopter has progressed to the point where learning to fly them is comparatively easy and loops and rolls are commonplace. Having reached that stage, from now on it really is up to you. It is possible to perform virtually *any* manoeuvre with a helicopter that can be performed by a fixed-wing aircraft. Several flyers have now demonstrated four point rolls and square loops, while there are rumours of inverted autorotations! Go to it.

The 'X-Cell' by *Miniature Aircraft USA* has become very popular in the USA. Originally produced in 0.50 and 0.61 powered versions, an 'X-Cell 30' is now available.

Not recommended to the average flyer is this kind of cramped flying space.

Chapter 11
Summary of control
requirements

ASSUMING that you have a fully
dedicated helicopter radio with
several pitch curves, rate
switches, and a gyro with two gain
settings controlled from the transmitter,
the following is a summary of the
various settings required for competing
in an FAI F3C contest.

Start-up and general flying

Throttle
Full range from full power (high) to stop
(low). Lower end set to required idle
speed by means of throttle trim.

Pitch
Approximately –3° (low) to +7° (high)
with +4° to +5° at the mid point of the
throttle stick. Pitch curve selector
switch, where fitted, in 'normal' (N)
position.

Cyclic
Set to give adequate control for flying
circuits. Rate switches at 'high' or 'low'
position to personal taste.

Tail
As for cyclic controls.

Gyro
Set to high gain.

ATS
Set as required to prevent tail swinging
in high rate of ascent and descent.

Hovering

Throttle
Full power (high) to hover speed (low).
Ideal setting should give constant speed
throughout pitch range. It may be
necessary to restrict full power (high)
setting to achieve this.

Pitch
From a high setting slightly less than
normal to a low setting of zero or slightly
positive. Mid point as for general flying.
Pitch curve selector switch in 'idle-up 1'
position.

Cyclic
Minimum possible movement for
adequate control. Rate switches in 'low'
position.

Tail
As for cyclic controls.

Gyro
Set to highest gain possible without causing tail oscillation.

ATS
Set to eliminate tail swing.

Aerobatics

Throttle
As for hovering but full throttle must be available.

Pitch
High setting to maximum possible value without causing loss of RPM in forward flight. Some loss acceptable in vertical climb. Low setting to suit aerobatic technique – usually –2° to –3°. Mid point as for general flying. Pitch curve selector switch in 'idle-up 2' position.

Cyclic
Sufficient movement to permit required rolling and looping rate. Rate switches in 'high' position.

Tail
As much movement as possible for stall turn and top hat manoeuvres. If rate switch is available and easily accessible, it can be switched to 'high' for these figures and low for all others.

Gyro
Set to low gain.

ATS
Switched off if possible.

Autorotation

Throttle
Switched to low idle for practice or motor stopped for contests. hold switch in 'on' position.

Pitch
Maximum possible range from maximum positive (high) to at least –3° or –5° to –6° with experience. Mid point as for general flying.

The latest *Heim* machine for FAI competition is the 'Lockheed'. High mounted tail rotor gives excellent rolling performance. Design is based on a prototype full-sized machine of which only one was built.

Cyclic
Rate switches in 'high' position.

Tail
Not effective or set to zero pitch if tail is still mechanically connected to main rotor.

Gyro
Not effective

ATS
Not effective.

Note that the mid point of the pitch range remains the same for all situations and all positions of the pitch curve selector switch. Where it is necessary to alter the position of the pitch curve selector switch in flight, this will normally be done with the throttle stick around the mid point. If there is any difference at this point it will give unwanted changes of height when the switch is operated. This also ensures that there will be no dramatic change in the 'feel' of the model at this critical point.

Some flyers are able to operate the gyro gain switch during flight to suit various manoeuvres. This is also done with the rate switches in some cases. Where 'hovering pitch' and 'hovering throttle' controls are available, it is possible to adjust these in flight also.

This type of operation is very much dependent on the individual flyer and his abilities. While some can utilise all of the equipment's facilities to the full, others are flirting with disaster when operating anything other than the basic control sticks in flight. When you are sufficiently competent, you must decide for yourself.

Some of the latest radios allow you to set the rates and trims automatically when the pitch curve switch (now also called the 'flight mode switch') is operated. This is a very useful facility, but currently very costly.

Subscribe now...
here's 3 good reasons why!

Within each issue these three informative magazines provide the expertise, and inspiration you need to keep abreast of developments in the exciting field of model aviation.

With regular new designs to build, practical features that take the mysteries out of construction, reports and detailed descriptions of the techniques and ideas of the pioneering aircraft modellers all over the world – they respresent three of the very best reasons for taking out a subscription. You need never miss a single issue or a single minute of aeromodelling pleasure again!

SUBSCRIPTION RATES

	U.K.	Europe	Middle East	Far East	Rest of World
RCM&E *Published monthly*	£16.80	£22.80	£23.00	£25.30	£23.40
Radio Modeller *Published monthly*	£16.80	£22.40	£22.60	£24.80	£23.00
Aeromodeller *Published monthly*	£23.40	£28.20	£28.40	£30.20	£28.70

Airmail Rates on Request

Your remittance with delivery details should be sent to:

The Subscriptions Manager **(CG51)**
Argus Specialist Publications
Argus House
Boundary Way
Hemel Hempstead
Herts
HP2 7ST